Primary
Design and Technology

A Guide for
Teacher Assistants

On the cover: Puppet design by Lucy Pavey (Y3), Cheddar County First School, Somerset

First published in 1996 by DATA
The Design and Technology Association
16 Wellesbourne.House, Walton Road,
Wellesbourne, Warwickshire CV35 9JB
© Copyright DATA
ISBN 1 898788 20 0

Contents

Foreword

The Design and Technology Association (DATA) is the recognised professional association for teachers and lecturers in design and technology. It is also an educational charity with the purpose of promoting and enhancing design and technology.

DATA is delighted to offer this publication to teacher assistants in primary schools. The booklet stems from research carried out as part of the DATA Survey of Design and Technology in Schools 1995/6. This research showed that 52% of schools had teacher assistants helping with the teaching of design and technology. These included full time paid staff, voluntary parent helpers, local industrialists and students. Clearly, with design and technology being a relatively new subject it is important that teacher assistants are aware of what the subject is trying to achieve and how they can help a busy teacher.

The booklet is designed to be read at leisure by teacher assistants so that they will be better informed of the context in which they are working. It may be photocopied by the purchasing school, and sections may be added to the school's own guidance for teacher assistants.

DATA believes that as teachers and their helpers become increasingly aware of the potential of design and technology both the quality of teaching and learning and children's motivation and enjoyment will grow. DATA would welcome feedback and suggestions about where further help could be provided.

DATA has a wide range of other primary products including *Guidance Materials for Key Stages 1&2* with Units of Work, the *Technical Vocabulary for Key Stages 1&2* booklet and the *Design and Technology Primary Coordinators' File.*

Finally, DATA would like to thank Julie Mantell for writing this booklet, as well as the many teacher assistants who have commented on it.

Andrew M Breckon
Chief Executive, DATA

Introduction

This booklet has been written to support anyone who is involved in helping children to take part in and improve their capability in design and technology. For the purpose of this booklet 'teacher assistants' are defined as adults who work (salaried or voluntarily) in school, often with children, but who are not employed as teachers.

Design and technology is a practical subject, one which encourages children to think and do, to try out and reflect. This type of activity can be very time consuming for teachers and therefore extra help is often welcomed in the classroom.

Teacher assistants are often keen to learn more and improve their skills and understanding. You may be an experienced teacher assistant or someone just starting out. You may have a particular expertise to offer in design and technology or you may not even really be sure what it is! It is important to remember that design and technology is still a relatively new area of the curriculum for children in primary school and we are still finding out about what children can achieve.

This booklet has been written to help you feel more confident in making a contribution to children's learning in this area. It will provide you with practical advice and give you the opportunity to extend your understanding of design and technology. However, the booklet is no substitute for advice given by the school's coordinator for design and technology or the class teacher.

The booklet is in five sections:

1. **Working in school**
2. **What is design and technology?**
3. **Why is design and technology important?**
4. **Supporting teaching and learning in design and technology**
5. **Extending your understanding of design and technology**

Whatever your experience to date read the booklet to make sure that you are clear about what design and technology is and how you can help children to get better at it.

1. Working in school

Every school is different and has different priorities and ways of working. You may already know what these are if you are familiar with the school where you work. If not you will need to find out what they are so that you can support teachers and children in the best way possible. It is important that the work that you do is pulling in the same direction as the rest of the school.

Some schools have guidelines for teacher assistants and offer training; in other schools, time will need to be set aside to discuss the way in which you are going to work. The nature of the support you will be giving will depend upon your role. You may be working in the school as a salaried member of staff, a voluntary helper or someone who has been invited into the school to share a particular expertise with the children.

Primary school teachers are very busy and there is little time available to discuss matters when the children are in the classroom. If you are going to be working with a teacher on a regular basis ask if you can have a meeting to discuss ways of working and to find out any necessary information.

> The classroom teacher will help you by:
> - giving clear instructions for specific tasks
> - providing advice on how to carry out tasks.

If you are going to do much work in design and technology then you will need to have a meeting with the design and technology coordinator. This is the teacher responsible for organising design and technology throughout the school.

> The coordinator will be able to help you with the following areas:
> - the school's policy for design and technology
> - the correct way of using tools
> - health and safety guidelines
> - where to find materials, tools and equipment
> - where to find other resources for design and technology.

Good communication is the key to successful working relationships. Find out what is expected of you and the 'dos' and 'don'ts' of how you work right from the start. Remember that it is the teacher who has the professional and legal responsibility for the children and that you work under their direction.

Good communication is a two way process and it is important for you to share information with the teacher. The teacher will want to know:
- your particular interests and areas of expertise
- any areas of skill or knowledge that you want to develop
- any concerns that you have about your work.

Tips for working with the teacher:

- find out what is expected of you
- ask if you are not sure of something
- don't intrude or take over – remember you are working under the teacher's direction
- arrive early to allow time to speak to the teacher
- be discreet – information about individual children should be treated as confidential
- give feedback that might be useful to the teacher.

Providing the working relationship is right, teacher assistants can be an invaluable resource for the busy teacher. Children will benefit from the extra help, attention and contact with other adults and hopefully you will enjoy it too!

2. What is design and technology?

Design and technology involves children learning about the made world around them through studying things which have been designed and made, and designing and making things themselves with a variety of materials.

The 'things' which children design and make are 'products' and are designed and made for a particular purpose and user or group of users. For example, drinks for a hot day, a moving storybook for young children, a bag to keep something safe.

Sometimes the products which children design and make are the real thing and can be used and evaluated – for instance they can try out the drinks they make. At other times the product will be a model of a new idea – for instance a machine for lifting a heavy load.

What's in a name?

There have been lots of names used over the years to describe practical making activities for children of primary school age such as junk model-ling, craft, sewing, cooking, cutting and sticking and model making. This may cause you to think, 'I used to do that at school, so what's new?' 'Isn't design and technology just a grander title for the same thing?'

Well no, although design and technology does involve children in making things, children need to do a lot more thinking than before and they need to make their own decisions rather than following a simple 'recipe' for making something.

To explain let's look at the experience of Jack who is 8 years old.

Jack's class has just finished a design and technology project in which the children have been designing and making glove puppets.

His teacher showed the children how to use a simple paper pattern and arranged for them to practise simple stitching and find out different ways of joining fabric and trimmings.

The class made a collection of glove and finger puppets, looked at how they had been made and thought about who they had been designed for. Handling the puppets and talking about them helped the children with their own ideas.

Jack designed an owl puppet for his sister who collects owls. He made it in paper first to check the size and shape and then from fabric having made a few changes to his original idea. When he had finished it, he made a drawing to show the different parts of the puppet and how he had made it.

So what did Jack learn?

Through this project Jack improved his **skills** in:
- stitching
- making things the right size
- cutting and shaping paper and fabric
- working with textiles
- planning his work.

Jack improved his **know how** about:
- using paper patterns
- how textile products are made.

Jack designed and made a product that was suitable for the user, his sister, in that she liked it, it fitted her hand and there was enough room for her to be able to move the wings and head. He was able to put his own ideas into it and create something he wanted to whilst learning how to design and make in textile materials. Through looking at other examples of puppets Jack found out the importance of having a seam allowance and also ideas for ways of adding colour and pattern to fabric.

In this example you can see that design and technology involves making things but it also requires children to:
- have ideas
- make decisions about what to make taking into account who it is for, what to use, how it will look, how it will work etc.
- try out ideas to see what will work well
- learn how to organise their time and the resources they use
- think of other ways of solving a problem when something doesn't work as they had planned
- learn about how things are made in the world around them.

During their time at primary school children will carry out a variety of design and technology projects. Each one will be designed to help the children get better at the things in the list above but the projects won't all look the same.

Children will be working with different materials, for instance – card, paper, reclaimed materials, wood strip, plastic, fabric, threads, food, construction kits and materials that can be moulded like clay, plasticine and papier mâché.

Some projects will help children to learn about using mechanisms or electrical circuits or how to make strong and stable structures.

As you can see, design and technology is very broad, and both boys and girls will have opportunities to work with the full range of materials.

So design and technology is much more than 'cutting and sticking', although that is an important part of it – otherwise things will come apart!

Design and technology is part of the National Curriculum for all children of primary school age in England and Wales. The National Curriculum sets out what children will experience at different stages. There is more information about this in Section 5: 'Extending your understanding of design and technology'.

3. Why is design and technology important?

Have you ever looked at what children do in school nowadays and thought how different it is from when you were at school? Have you ever wondered why it has changed, why children need to learn all these different things?

Technology is part of our world

There are lots of reasons for these changes but a central one is that, quite simply, life is different now and is changing all the time. We are all adapting the way we organise our lives as a result of the developments in technology. Design has brought about some changes and found new ways of applying new technology to change or world. Every day we handle materials and products that were not widely available, or hadn't even been thought of fifty years ago.

Think about how technology has changed the way your life is today from that of people fifty years ago, for example:
- you can buy clothes made out of newly developed fabrics which are easy to care for or have different characteristics – e.g. Lycra for close fitting garments
- household equipment such as automatic washing machines, fridge freezers, microwaves, televisions, videos and telephones are commonplace and are much more sophisticated
- shopping has been made easier with supermarkets, mail order, open all hours shops
- foods are packaged in different ways to keep them fresh for longer
- there is a greater choice of products to buy
- recycling banks are available for waste paper, bottles and cans
- cars have been developed to be more efficient and comfortable and many have been adapted to cause less pollution
- computers are smaller and faster and are used by many people at work and in the home
- there are more effective drugs and treatments for medical conditions, e.g. laser surgery.

Design and technology develops skills and knowledge

One of the purposes of education is to help children to make sense of their world and to be capable in what they do. Learning design and technology at school will help them to do that.

Learning design and technology is also important in that it helps to prepare children for living and working in the 21st century. Although technology has been part of our lives since the very first tools were made by early man, the pace and number of developments has increased dramatically in recent times. To cope in the future children will need to have a greater understanding of technology and be more adaptable to change.

We are all consumers of technology and therefore will need to be able to use it and make choices about it, e.g. learning how to use the new telephone services or making the best choice when shopping for furniture. When choosing which product to buy you will be involved in asking the same kinds of questions that children do in design and technology:

- Do I like it? Is it what I need?
- Is it the right size, shape, pattern, colour?
- Is it easy to care for?
- Is it strong and sturdy?
- Is it safe?
- Is it value for money?

Technology can bring many improvements to our lives but can also have other effects, e.g. environmental damage, changes in employment. It is more important than ever before that children are educated to make sensible decisions about the use of technology.

The ability to design and to think through practical problems will be useful in many situations - from planning a children's party to decorating a house, from planning a holiday to starting a new project at work. Design and technology is relevant to all of us - not just professional designers and technologists. It develops skills which we all need in our daily lives.

Design and technology is a good way of learning other things

Have you ever noticed how children enjoy designing and making things? This is because many children enjoy learning by doing. Children will often respond to design and technology in a positive way because it is practical and they are able to follow through their own ideas.

Many teachers take advantage of the opportunity for children to use design and technology activities as a way of learning or practising skills and knowledge from other subject areas, e.g. measuring, writing, drawing, finding out information from books, scientific testing, learning about forces and energy.

Design and technology helps children to:
- have a better understanding of the world around them
- improve their own ability to design and make
- learn how to organise themselves
- solve practical problems
- be creative in their thinking and doing
- learn about how things are made
- learn about different technologies.

4. Supporting teaching and learning in design and technology

As a teacher assistant you might be asked to support in design and technology in a number of different ways. This section takes a closer look at some of the activities that you might be involved in and provides some practical advice about how to go about them:

a) showing children how to do something
b) talking to children while they are working
c) supporting practical work
d) supervising a group working
e) organising and maintaining resources
f) creating a display

Remember that it is very important to discuss with the class teacher what is expected of you and ask if you are unsure. Being clear to start with can prevent misunderstandings and will make your support more effective.

a) Showing children how to do something

As a teacher assistant you may be required to demonstrate something, for example, how to use a piece of equipment such as a glue gun or a sewing machine, or how to do a particular technique, such as make a simple pop up or print on fabric.

This might be as part of your work as a general assistant or you might have been invited into the classroom specially for this as it is your area of expertise. It might be a long or short activity, with a group of children or with individuals. Whatever the circumstances, you may find some of the tips below helpful.

One of the key things about demonstrating is to get and maintain the children's attention and involve them in ways which will help them to take in what it is you are demonstrating.

Tips for showing children how to do something

- Make sure that the group size is right – if there are too many children then do it twice with smaller groups
- Position yourself and the children so that they can see clearly
- Avoid having the children facing anything distracting – e.g. *another group doing something else*
- Explain what you are doing simply and clearly – don't rush what you are saying and make sure that all the children can hear you
- Try to look around the group from time to time to get eye contact
- Ask questions to engage the children's attention... e.g. *What do you think this is for?, What do you think happens next? Why do you think I am holding it this way? Why don't I hold it like this? What do you think I would need to do if I wanted to make a bigger hole?*
- Emphasise significant points by looking up and repeating them or bringing their attention to it... *do you see this?*....perhaps holding up what you are doing
- Involve the children by allowing them to touch, handle, look, smell, listen, ... whatever is appropriate to the situation
- Ask individual children to help you – *to hold something, to fetch something, to measure, to choose.....etc.*
- Get the children to repeat something, e.g. *a new word, or recap - –Who can remember what this is called? What did I do first?*
- When you have finished it is a good idea to go back over what you have shown them and check that they understand.

Preparation

Whatever you are demonstrating - whether it is simple or complex, whether it takes one minute or ten, think through how you are going to do it. Don't be afraid to practise what you are going to do; teachers often practise if they are unsure.

- What are the important points for the children to know?
- Are there health and safety guidelines you should tell them?
- Are there particular rules associated with this activity?
- Where will the children be?
- Do you have ready everything you need?

b) Talking to children while they are working

Learning to talk fluently and to listen to others is a very important part of children's work in primary school. Having other adults in the classroom can help children to develop their speaking and listening skills as well as the other activities they are involved in.

Talking to the children while they are working is a very common task given to teacher assistants and one which, if done well, can make a significant difference to children's learning and success in the activity. But not everyone finds it easy to know what to say. Here are a few ideas:

Questions

Use questions that encourage children to think and reflect about what they are doing. There are lots of different types of questions and reasons for asking them. When you are talking to children try to include questions which require more than a one word answer – questions which begin with *Why...*, *What do you think...*, *What would happen if... ?* are useful for this.

The following questions might be used when helping children in design and technology. The ones you choose will naturally depend upon the age of the children and the activity they are involved in:

Questions to help them in designing:
Who is it for?
What size does it need to be?
What could you use?
What else would work/could you use?
How are you going to make it?
How is it going to work?
What would happen if you.......?
How could you.......?

Questions to help them organise themselves:
What are you going to do next/first?
What will you need?
Where are you going to work?
Who will you work with?
Who is doing what in your group?

Questions to help them make choices:
Which do you prefer?
Which would work best?

Questions to help them think about making:
What tool would be the best to do that?
How are you going to join those pieces together?
What could you use?
How could you make those the right size?
How are you going to decorate it?
How could you make that part look better?
How could you make it stronger?

Questions to help them evaluate a product:
What does it need to do?
Who is it for?
How does it work?
What would make it better?

Statements
Don't be afraid to express an opinion or share your own experiences which might be relevant to what the children are doing. e.g. *I prefer the taste of this yoghurt – it isn't as sweet as that one and I like the pieces of fruit in it, they give it an interesting texture, I had a card for my birthday which worked a bit like that - it had a window cut out and a picture behind.*

Point things out that might help the children to have a greater appreciation of the made world around them. This might be during a design and technology lesson or on an informal occasion. e.g. *Look at the way that has been joined together, What a lovely pattern on the back of your jacket – haven't they done that carefully.*

When commenting on children's work be positive and give praise where you can see a child has worked well. Don't give praise inappropriately - it is important that it is something that is recognised as worth having. If you praise everything any child does you won't help them to achieve their best. Help the children to see what they could do to make their work even better.

Tips for talking to children

- Try not to let children take up all your time talking about what happened at playtime or what they saw on television last night.
- Try to talk to all the children involved in the activity not just the dominant ones.
- Try to get the right balance when talking – too much and you can distract the children from what they are trying to do or interfere too much so that they don't sort things out for themselves.
- Listen to what they say – it will give you valuable information about what they understand and how they are getting on with the task
- Show an interest and enthusiasm in your tone of voice and body language as well as in the words you say.
- Try to use the correct vocabulary (DATA has a small booklet, *Technical Vocabulary for Key Stages 1&2*, which may be helpful.)

c) Supporting practical work

This will involve helping in various ways and may include preparing materials, demonstrating how to do something and talking to the children while they are working.

It is very important to remember that design and technology encourages children to be 'capable' so you must help children to do things for themselves. Sometimes you will come across children who would rather you did everything for them – *Will you draw this for me?, I can't do this, you do it....etc.* In these circumstances it is important to be firm and clear in your own mind about whose work it is. Sometimes guiding children by talking them through it can be enough support.

If you are the kind of person who likes designing and making things you may be tempted to do it for them. Well DON'T! It's their work, not yours and if you interfere you won't be helping them to get better at design and technology.

Occasionally you may be required to do something for a child if a dangerous or difficult tool is needed. This might be appropriate if there are no other solutions to the problem, e.g. *using a hot glue gun, an iron to fix a design on fabric, taking a hot tin out of the oven.* You may need to support some children when carrying out a skill for the first time or when they lack confidence or know-how.

Watching and listening will be a very important part of your work – it will tell you what is really going on, who needs help and what kind of help they need.

Tips for helping children in practical work

- Don't do things for them that they can do for themselves, e.g. *fetch materials, clear away, use tools*
- Encourage them to think about what they are doing and to work carefully
- Remind the children about safe working
- Follow the same rules as the children when using tools or they will soon copy bad habits .
- Encourage them to keep their work area tidy, *e.g. return tools and equipment which are no longer needed, put unusable scraps in the bin, rearrange equipment and materials on the table so that it is easier to work*
- Encourage them to be as accurate as possible, *e.g. cutting carefully, measuring food ingredients, marking the position before punching a hole or sticking something down*
- Watch how the children are holding tools and how they have positioned themselves and suggest changes if necessary, *e.g. you might find it easier to stand up to do that, try holding it like this, use this finger to guide it/keep it still*
- Make sure that girls and boys have equal access to tools and equipment – sometimes that is true in theory but not in practice!
- If you need to show a child how to do something, use a spare piece of material rather than their work
- Use the correct names for tools, equipment and materials and help the children to remember them.

d) Supervising a group working

The classroom teacher is always ultimately responsible for the children. However there may be occasions when you are asked to supervise a group of children doing an activity perhaps when they are working in a practical area outside the classroom.

Make sure that you know what the teacher wants from you and the children for that particular activity. What are the learning objectives? How much time is there? What about clearing away? Are there any particular rules for working in that area or with those materials?

Be quiet but firm with the children. Wait until they are all quiet before you speak – don't allow interruptions to succeed. Make sure that children use tools and equipment carefully and safely - the majority of children will act sensibly in these circumstances but if you have an exception and safety is compromised then refer to the teacher.

Encourage the children to take care of their working environment, e.g. *return tools when they have used them, keep working surfaces tidy.* You can often help the children to do this by giving them a particular place to put things, e.g. *a box for scrap pieces of wood, a shallow tray or piece of coloured card on the table to keep tools or components in.*

The class teacher will give you specific guidance about ways of working but here are some general tips you may find useful:

Tips for safe working

- encourage the children to keep their work area organised
- discourage unnecessary movement around the room
- closely supervise the use of any potentially hazardous tools
- don't let children queue next to potentially hazardous tools and equipment
- watch for sharp things and hot things
- remind children about the safe use of tools and equipment.

Tips for clearing away

- leave enough time for the children to do it
- organise resources so that children know where to return equipment, materials, models, unfinished work etc.
- make sure that all children are involved and not just the same ones every time. Giving children specific tasks can help to cajole most children, e.g. *pick up ten scraps from the floor, wipe the tables, collect the scissors.*
- if children have unfinished models make sure all the bits are kept together - e.g. *use masking tape to attach loose pieces to the model, keep pieces together in an envelope or resealable bag, pin pieces of fabric together*
- make sure that children have named their work in an appropriate way, e.g. *writing their name on the back, using a sticky label, writing on a piece of masking tape, pinning a label on to fabric*

e) Organising and maintaining resources

Having well organised resources which work when you need them is important for the smooth running of any design and technology activity. Most schools have a teacher who is responsible for coordinating design and technology and this will be an aspect of his/her role. Many coordinators work with teacher assistants to help them to carry out this task.

The coordinator may ask you to help with tidying up and sorting out, unpacking new stock when it arrives, checking equipment, cleaning or preparing materials for use. If you have been asked to take on this technician's role, the following tips might help:

Tips for organising and maintaining resources

- check with the coordinator what is expected of you and if there are any guidelines for organising and maintaining equipment
- remember that a good storage system means that people can quickly find what they are looking for and return things to the right place
- containers such as drawers, boxes, cartons should be clearly labelled and the right size for the job. If children are using the storage system the labels should use appropriate print or perhaps have a small sample of the contents stuck on the side for non-readers
- shadow boards are useful for tools
- think about ways of storing sharp tools so that they are secure and people won't hurt themselves getting them out
- make sure that storage containers are stable and cannot be knocked over easily
- containers with compartments can be very useful for sorting things out - *e.g. a components box, a large box with smaller containers inside it.*

f) Creating displays

Displays serve a number of different purposes in the classroom. As well as looking attractive, displays can be used to:
- present information to children
- stimulate their curiosity
- give value to children's work
- share ideas.

In design and technology displays might include:
- children's work – e.g. *models, drawings, questionnaires, prototypes, plans, writing*
- products – e.g. *a collection of containers or moving toys, products made from the same materials - textiles, plastic, an old sewing machine with the cover removed so that the children can see what is inside*
- published information – e.g. *posters, pictures, books, magazines, statements*
- materials and simple tools that children can try out.

If you are asked to create a display the teacher will give you guidance on how it should be done. Some schools have a written display policy which might be useful. There is a lot of information published about display – the following tips provide a few ideas and points to remember.

Tips for display:

- make sure you know how to use any equipment correctly – e.g. *the paper trimmer to get proper right angles, stapler, spray glue*
- try not to include too much or the display will look cluttered
- make sure that the display is at the right height for the children
- avoid using fixings which detract from what you are displaying – e.g. *drawing pins*
- before attaching 2-dimensional work with staples or pins, lay it out temporarily with Blutack so that it is easier to make changes if necessary
- when displaying 3-dimensional work arrange it on coloured card or fabric to improve the effect. Cardboard boxes of different sizes can be placed under fabric to make platforms of different heights.
- show that you value the children's work by the way that you handle it
- think about the purpose of the display and who it is for. Think about any practical difficulties – e.g. *if it is next to the sink or a busy thoroughfare.*

Involving children in displaying work can be a good opportunity for them to practise designing. If you are asked to help children display their own work encourage them to think about what they are doing, who it is for, what the possibilities are and how they could do it well.

5. Extending your understanding of design and technology

This section explains more about what children need to learn in design and technology. As they progress through the school they will develop an increasing repertoire of skills and knowledge that they can use to improve their designing and making. It is rather like learning new words and ways of writing so that they can write better stories.

The information below explains the types of activity and the skills and knowledge that children will experience in design and technology.

1. Types of activity

In design and technology children will be involved in different types of activity which have different purposes and opportunities for learning:

a)   designing and making – this provides children with opportunities to improve their ability in designing and making.

> Examples:
> * *designing and making a rainhat for teddy might involve the children in experimenting with materials, sizes and shapes, making and testing their rainhat*
> * *designing and making a moving toy might involve the children in having ideas, trying them out, planning, making and evaluating and applying their understanding about mechanisms and materials*
> * *designing and making a healthy sandwich might involve the children in researching what people like, trying out different bread products, learning how to work with tools, planning, making and evaluating.*

b) focused practical tasks – these activities help children to learn new skills and techniques that can be used in their designing and making.

> Examples:
> * *how to do backstitch to join two pieces of fabric together*
> * *how to cut dowel to make axles*
> * *how to use the measuring equipment for working with food*

c) working with products – this type of activity helps children to understand the made world around them and can also be a useful source of ideas for their designing and making. It can help them to develop understanding about how materials are used, how structures and mechanisms work and how products are designed to meet people's needs.

> Example:
> *Children looking at a collection of shoes might be asked:*
> * *What type of person/activity has this shoe been designed for?*
> * *How can you tell?*
> * *What is the difference between the baby's shoe and the trainer?*
> * *What are the parts of the shoe? What is each part for?*
> * *What fastenings have been used?*
> * *Which parts of a shoe need to be very strong?*
> * *Why do you think this shoe is made out of this material?*
> * *Which would be a good shoe for wearing on the beach, running, to a party, in the rain?*

2.   Skills

a) Designing skills

Designing involves children in finding out about what needs to be done, having ideas, developing and communicating their ideas, planning and evaluating.

When young children are designing they will often be designing and making at the same time. It is through handling the materials that many of their ideas come.

> Example:
> *when designing a playground for some play people, a cardboard tube might suggest a tunnel to crawl through, an orange net might become a net for scrambling on.*

As children become more experienced they need to be encouraged to try things out and to make more informed choices. They might develop their ideas through talking, rearranging materials, making a prototype, drawing or making a model from a construction kit. As they progress they will increasingly take into account what other people need and like. They will become more capable in planning ahead and judging how good their ideas are.

b) Making skills

Supporting children in developing their making skills will involve helping them to get better at:

working with materials – as they progress they will need to improve their skills in:

- measuring and marking out, e.g. *marking where to punch a hole, using a paper pattern, measuring liquids*
- cutting and shaping, e.g. *using scissors, a hacksaw, folding paper*
- joining and combining, e.g. *sewing, using a glue stick, stapler*
- finishing, e.g. *painting, adding pieces of coloured paper, covering in card, glazing a piece of clay work.*

planning – as they progress children should become more able to organise themselves and think ahead:

> *What will we need? What should we do first? How could we do this part?*

evaluating – as they progress they will need to reflect upon their work and make judgements about it:

> *How well does it work? How could we improve the way it...looks, tastes, feels, fits? Did we make the best use of materials – e.g. is it covered in sticky tape when glue would have been better?*

3. Knowledge and understanding

a) Materials and components

Children need to learn how to work with materials and how to choose the most appropriate material for the task in hand. There are opportunities in most design and technology activities for children to think about materials and to learn more about how they are used.

When working with the children encourage them to talk about the properties and qualities of the materials using a range of words to describe them.

> *e.g. bendy, stiff, strong, stretchy, waterproof, transparent, smooth, soft, shiny, colourful*

When looking at products children should be encouraged to think about the materials which have been used for different parts and to think about why those materials have been chosen.

> Example:
> *when looking at a chair children might observe a plastic seat, metal legs, plastic stoppers on the bottom of the legs to prevent scratching the floor, metal fixings, a fabric covered cushion. Why have these materials been selected? What would it be like if it had wooden legs / a metal cushion etc.?*

Children also need to learn the names of materials, components and the tools which are used to work with them.

The following list describes some of the materials that children use in design and technology:

construction materials
Children learn about the use of different construction materials in the world around them. Children design and make with a range of construction materials including:

- sheet materials – e.g. paper, card, cardboard, corrugated plastic, polythene sheet
- items that can be assembled to make products – e.g. cardboard tubes, cartons, plastic bottles, cotton reels, corks, foil dishes
- materials for making frameworks – e.g. straws, paper sticks, dowel, twigs, square section wood, wire
- mouldable materials – e.g. plasticine, playdough, clay, papier mâché.

construction kits

Children use construction kits to learn a variety of things in the primary classroom. In design and technology children use them to:

- make different kinds of structure – e.g. walls, arches, bridges, towers
- learn about mechanisms such as pulleys and gears
- improve skills in assembling components and following instructions
- make models of their ideas.

mechanical and electrical components

In some projects children use components such as wheels, pulleys, gears, batteries, bulbs and buzzers.

textiles

Children use textile materials such as fabrics, threads and trimmings in design and technology. They learn about how textiles are used in the world around them and design and make products that have a particular purpose for a user or group of users. Children need to work with materials that they can cut and join themselves. Links with Art can be developed through exploring pattern making and techniques such as fabric painting, printing, weaving and batik.

food

Children learn about food products and work with food ingredients in their designing and making. Children need to learn about safe and hygienic ways of working. If you are supporting children in working with food make sure you know your school's guidelines for food work.

b) Control

In some design and technology activities children learn how to control products using mechanisms and simple electrical circuits.

- Mechanisms include simple moving joints, pop ups, levers, wheels and axles, pulleys, gears etc.
- Electrical control involves children learning how to use simple switches and use components such as bulbs, buzzers and motors in their products.

c) Structures

In design and technology children learn about different ways of making structures:

> Example:
> *making a frame and covering it in fabric or card (like a kite or a tent), moulding (as in papier mâché over a balloon), making a net to construct a box, weaving.*

They learn ways of making things stable:

> Example:
> *having a wide base (as in a music stand or traffic cone) and how to strengthen and reinforce their products, e.g. adding another layer of material, adding a triangular support.*

d) Products and applications

Children learn about how products have been designed and made. They handle them, look carefully at the materials used and how they have been put together and judge how well they work.

e) Quality

Children need to think about quality in their own work and when looking at products. When supporting children help them to think about quality in terms of fitness for purpose as well as how well the product is made.

> Example:
> *when looking at a book designed for younger children, Is it sturdy? Is it attractive and interesting for young children? Does it have the right amount of words and pictures? Is it well made?*

f) Health and safety

Health and safety is an important part of design and technology. Children need to be shown the correct way of using tools, equipment and materials and learn how to be safe when working in design and technology. Make sure that you know any health and safety guidelines including the rules that the children should follow, the correct use of tools and hygiene when working with food.

Children should also think about health and safety in products.

e.g. covering over the sharp ends of paper fasteners if they might cause injury.

g) Vocabulary

Children need to learn the correct words for tools, materials and techniques in design and technology. Whenever you are working with the children introduce them to new words and encourage them to use a wide range of vocabulary. Make sure you know the correct names so you can help the children.

DATA has produced a small booklet: *Technical vocabulary for KS1&2* which outlines essential vocabulary for design and technology. Your school may have a copy that you can look at.

Where to find out more

We hope that you have found this booklet useful. If you want to find out more about design and technology why not try some of the following:

- the design and technology coordinator in your school
- training courses for teacher assistants
- written materials in school, e.g.
  - school guidelines
  - books on techniques and use of tools
  - DATA publications:

    ❏ **Technical vocabulary for KS1&2**
    This booklet lists and explains design and technology vocabulary suitable for the primary school.

    ❏ sections of the **Primary Coordinators' File**
    This contains sections which may be useful to teacher assistants, e.g. health and safety, working with food, managing tools, equipment and materials.

    ❏ **Guidance Materials for Key Stages 1&2**
    This includes 30 units of work which provide a comprehensive range of pupil activities.

  - DfEE publications:

    ❏ the leaflet **Why Design and Technology?'***
    This leaflet explains to parents and other members of the community why design and technology is important. It is available free of charge from the Department for Education and Employment Tel: 0171 925 6146

  - SCAA publications:

    ❏ **Design and technology: the new requirements***
    This booklet explains the content of the National Curriculum for design and technology through practical examples.

Ask the design and technology coordinator for further details

Publications marked with an asterisk have been sent to all schools.

Other primary publications from DATA

The Design and Technology Primary Coordinators' File
This file covers all the areas for which a coordinator in primary schools is responsible, including management, curriculum planning, subject knowledge, health and safety. It also has space for the school's own written material.
Price: £12.50/£20.00 non-members

Guidance Materials for Design and Technology Key Stages 1&2
This DfEE supported pack contains a guide book with details on developing a policy for design and technology, course management, planning and monitoring. This comprehensive pack also includes 30 units of work, planning sheets, an assessment card, unit of work templates and a poster.
Price: £7.50/£13.50 non-members

Technical Vocabulary for Key Stages 1&2
A booklet containing essential vocabulary for design and technology at Key Stages 1 & 2. Over 500 key words and definitions.
Price: £5.00/£7.50 non-members

Guidance for Primary Phase Initial Teacher Training and Continuing Professional Development in Design and Technology – Competences for Newly Qualified and Practising Teachers
This detailed research paper is a major contribution to the process of identifying the content of training courses for design and technology in ITE.
Price: £5.00/£7.50 non-members